SIGNS YOUR S
IS DEAD

BY
JERRY KING

CCC PUBLICATIONS

Published by

CCC Publications
1111 Rancho Conejo Blvd.
Suites 411 & 412
Newbury Park, CA 91320

Manufactured in the United States of America

Cover ©1995 CCC Publications

Interior illustrations ©1995 CCC Publications

Cover & interior art by Jerry King

Cover/Interior production by Oasis Graphics

ISBN: 0-918259-82-7

If your local U.S. bookstore is out of stock, copies of this book may be obtained by mailing check or money order for $4.99 per book (plus $2.50 to cover postage and handling) to: CCC Publications; 111 Rancho Conejo Blvd.; Suites 411 & 412; Newbury Park, CA 91320

Pre-publication Edition – 5/95

The ugly blind date you've been fixed up with blows you off.

You spend thousands of dollars on a breast enlargement and the only thing you get is a sore back.

Women reject you even when you're minding your own business.

You can't even get sexually harassed by the pigs
standing near the water cooler.

You start watching soap operas just for the Feminine Commercials.

The 1-900 woman hangs up on you.

You make frequent visits to the doctor just for the physicals.

Sleazy day-time talk shows offer you big bucks to
exploit your sexual misfortunes to millions of viewers.

The worth of your dirty magazine collection
exceeds the amount of your car.

Some men get more men than you do.

You can't even get laid in a women's prison.

Your widowed Grandmother gets more dates than you do.

You join a Health Club with the hopes of scoring
only to be totally humiliated.

The stripper feels sorry for you and gives your money back.

Convicted serial killers get more girls than you do.

For some unknown reason, you've become a V.I.P. at the Porno Movie Theater.

The sight of your cat's litter makes you realize that even your pet gets more action than you.

You spend your life savings to hire a super model to act as your date at your class reunion so you don't go by yourself and look like a loser.

The ugly geek who madly loved you in high school rejects you.

You attend a sex addiction support group with the hopes of finding a nympho only to be rejected.

The prophylactic you keep in your wallet
crumbles to dust due to old age.

You call Dial-A-Date and lie about how rich and good-looking you are and still get rejected.

You purposely walk past a construction site with the hopes of getting a cat call only to be treated politely.

You try your darndest to look like a Rock Star to attract groupies,
but the only thing you wind up with is a ridiculous haircut.

Everytime your mom sees a child she breaks down and cries because she realizes you'll never make her a grandmother.

The Hooker you proposition suddenly finds religion.

You actually think Bay Watch is a good television show.

Your local singles bar has a restraining order put out against you.

The *'Use it or Lose it'* phrase becomes a horrifying reality.

Men actually use you for your mind.

Your definition of a romantic evening is a 'Spin Cycle.'

All women refer to you as "a really nice guy."

Everyone you've ever dated has turned gay.

Whenever you and your friends get together to share sexual stories, your only contribution is a good cry.

You donate your sperm because you have no use for it anyways.
And, you could use the fifty bucks.

In a personal ad, you describe yourself as a rich, sex-crazed blond who owns a liquor store and you still don't get a single response.

The adult section where you rent videos has been changed to your name in honor of your excellent patronage.

A woman claims that you being in her view
is a form of sexual harassment.

You're arrested for stealing a mannequin from a lingerie store.

You frequent strip clubs so often that you receive
holiday cards from them.

You start receiving junk mail from companies that
specialize in vibrators.

Every time you bring up the topic of your sex-life to your personal psychic you mysteriously get disconnected.

No longer is walking an old lady an act of kindness,
rather it's a cheap turn on.

You spend your entire paycheck getting a girl drunk so you'll look more attractive to her and the only thing that happens is that she throws up on you.

You make a pass at closing time ("when *every* girl *looks* prettier")
and still are rejected by a bleary-eyed drunk.

The only "Boobs" you encounter are your friends.

Sex therapists from all over the world pay you a large sum of money to help you with your pathetic sex-life, just for the challenge.

What would normally be a cheap ploy on other girls
is really the truth with you.

You get arrested for just thinking about having sex with someone.

The monastery votes you their "Man of the Year" and makes you an honorary member.

Absolutely, positively no movies on cable will be considered unless the warning "Nudity-Strong Sexual Content" follows the title.

You wear a tight skirt to attract men, but they never see you in it because you end up in the hospital to have it surgically removed.

Even the dog won't let you touch her.

The only person who thinks you're attractive
and will go out with you is your grandma.

The Playboy Channel isn't just another channel on cable,
it's a way of life.

Men claim *they* have the headache.

Your best friend sells the depressing details
of your sex-life to a national tabloid.

You give your showerhead its own name.

You come to realize that your standards have reached
an all-new low.

The phrase "*When hell freezes over*" is actually encouraging.

Even Madonna won't have sex with you.

Titles By CCC PUBLICATIONS

Retail $4.99
POSITIVELY PREGNANT
SIGNS YOUR SEX LIFE IS DEAD
WHY MEN DON'T HAVE A CLUE
40 AND HOLDING YOUR OWN
CAN SEX IMPROVE YOUR GOLF?
THE COMPLETE BOOGER BOOK
THINGS YOU CAN DO WITH A USELESS MAN
FLYING FUNNIES
MARITAL BLISS & OXYMORONS
THE VERY VERY SEXY ADULT
   DOT-TO-DOT BOOK
THE DEFINITIVE FART BOOK
THE COMPLETE WIMP'S GUIDE TO SEX
THE CAT OWNER'S SHAPE UP MANUAL
PMS CRAZED: TOUCH ME AND I'LL KILL YOU!
RETIRED: LET THE GAMES BEGIN
MALE BASHING: WOMEN'S FAVORITE PASTIME
THE OFFICE FROM HELL
FOOD & SEX
FITNESS FANATICS
YOUNGER MEN ARE BETTER THAN RETIN-A
BUT OSSIFER, IT'S NOT MY FAULT

Retail $4.95
1001 WAYS TO PROCRASTINATE
THE WORLD'S GREATEST PUT-DOWN LINES
HORMONES FROM HELL II

SHARING THE ROAD WITH IDIOTS
THE GREATEST ANSWERING MACHINE
   MESSAGES OF ALL TIME
WHAT DO WE DO NOW?? (A Guide For New
   Parents)
HOW TO TALK YOU WAY OUT OF A TRAFFIC
   TICKET
THE BOTTOM HALF (How To Spot Incompetent
   Professionals)
LIFE'S MOST EMBARRASSING MOMENTS
HOW TO ENTERTAIN PEOPLE YOU HATE
YOUR GUIDE TO CORPORATE SURVIVAL
THE SUPERIOR PERSON'S GUIDE TO
   EVERYDAY IRRITATIONS
GIFTING RIGHT

Retail $5.95
50 WAYS TO HUSTLE YOUR FRIENDS ($5.99)
HORMONES FROM HELL
HUSBANDS FROM HELL
KILLER BRAS & Other Hazards Of The 50's
IT'S BETTER TO BE OVER THE HILL THAN
   UNDER IT
HOW TO REALLY PARTY!!!
WORK SUCKS!
THE PEOPLE WATCHER'S FIRLD GUIDE
THE UNOFFICIAL WOMEN'S DIVORCE GUIDE
THE ABSOLUTE LAST CHANCE DIET BOOK

FOR MEN ONLY (How To Survive Marriage)
THE UGLY TRUTH ABOUT MEN
NEVER A DULL CARD
RED HOT MONOGAMY
   (In Just 60 Seconds A Day) ($6.95)

Retail $3.95
YOU KNOW YOU'RE AN OLD FART WHEN...
NO HANG-UPS
NO HANG-UPS II
NO HANG-UPS III
GETTING EVEN WITH THE ANSWERING
   MACHINE
HOW TO SUCCEED IN SINGLES BARS
HOW TO GET EVEN WITH YOUR EXES
TOTALLY OUTRAGEOUS BUMPER-SNICKERS
   ($2.95)

NO HANG-UPS – CASSETTES Retail $4.98

Vol. I:	GENERAL MESSAGES	(Female)
Vol. I:	GENERAL MESSAGES	(Male)
Vol. II:	BUSINESS MESSAGES	(Female)
Vol. II:	BUSINESS MESSAGES	(Male)
Vol. III:	'R' RATED MESSAGES	(Female)
Vol. III:	'R' RATED MESSAGES	(Male)
Vol. IV:	SOUND EFFECTS ONLY	
Vol. V:	CELEBRI-TEASE	